Education Champions: The Butterfly Effect

Dara A. Lehner

Editor

Name: Dara A. Lehner, Editor
Title: Education Champions
Subtitle: The Butterfly Effect

Identifiers:
LCCN: 2024937053
ISBN:979-8-9886992-6-2 paperback
ISBN: 979-8-9886992-7-9ebook
Subjects: 1. Memoir; 2. Education

Cover Photo : Dara Lehner
Cover Design by Kim Autrey and Dara Lehner

Published by
Pen and Pearls Publishing
Raeford, NC

Dedication

This book is to pay homage to all teachers who have given of themselves to encourage, inspire, and challenge their students to do their best in all they do, not just in their academic pursuits.

Most of these educators have never received a most deserving show of appreciation or gratitude for their diligence or sacrifices.

We dedicate this book to you, our unsung heroes, with our sincerest appreciation of how you shaped our lives.

Thank you!
~ The Authors

Contents

Acknowledgments

To all the teachers who are highlighted by the authors in this anthology. We value your contributions to all your students and communities in which you have taught.

To all the authors who believed in this project, and graciously shared your reflections and gratitude for a special teacher in your life.

To my family and friends who continue to encourage my perspective on quality and not settling for the status quo.

~ DAL

Introduction

Lately, education and many of those who teach have been subjected to ridicule, harassment, unwarranted supervision, and a desire to commandeer curriculums. This book will NOT address the politicizing of the education system. It is purely meant to pay tribute to all the selfless educators who have inspired so many.

I asked the authors in this book to reflect on their teachers and those who had made an impact on their lives. Other than a few basic instructions on the style sheet, word count, naming a file, etc., no further directions were given because I wanted their stories to be told.

What I found was an overarching theme throughout all the stories - the nurturing and concern shown in the guidance given. Also, the teachers didn't shelter students from work or struggle, much like a butterfly's emergence from a chrysalis. It's that struggle that makes a butterfly strong in its life journey.

Looking back on my schooling, I am blessed to have been taught by exceptional teachers. I can count on one hand those who I would have given a failing grade. As time went on, I pursued my educational credentials, and realized those few teachers had taught me valuable lessons in what I should not do as an educator.

I have written about two outstanding teachers, Miss Gertrude McFarland, in fourth grade, and Mr. Earl Kirkland, my high school Chemistry teacher, I am forever grateful to them.

This book has compiled stories that were authored by people who believe in showing gratitude to the unsung heroes in their lives. Some authors were educated in far-away places in the world, but most were primarily here in the United States. I am thrilled to be able to compile their stories to share with you.

I would encourage you to seek out teachers who deserve to be honored for their contributions and thank them personally or their families.

~ Dara Lehner

1

Mr. David Abby

Fifth-Grade Journeys

When thinking back on my journey through school, two teachers helped to mold, encourage, and inspire me. That's right, not just one, but two! And you know what? They were both men.

For this writing, however, I am going to tell you about just one of them. There is too much to say about each of them for just one appreciation.

With that said, in the fifth grade I fondly remember Mr. David Abby. He always made everyone feel welcomed and appreciated. Mr. Abby also exuded values and morals when instructing our unformed minds. He would always speak on our level and was very fair. As a matter of fact, I remember while taking a certain test I was looking over the shoulder at the paper of the person in front of me because I didn't know the answer to a question. Yes, I was cheating! (This was before I learned to be more honest and have integrity.) Well, unbeknownst to me Mr. Abby was coming up from behind me and saw I was cheating. All he said was, " You're done. Bob!". To which he simply grabbed my paper, crumpled it up in his hands, and tossed it into the garbage. Not ONE word was said about that incident to me ever again. Needless to say, I learned a very valuable lesson!

Although numerous times stand out in my memory of the fifth grade there was one other event that shines above them all, expressing Mr. Abby's generosity. Three of us in class won a spelling bee, taking first, second, and third place. To celebrate, Mr. Abby, on his own, took the three of us in his beautiful convertible to a place called Deer Forest in Coloma, Michigan. Deer Forest was an enchanting place, full of animals that would eat out of your hand, (and yes, there were lots of deer).

Mr. Abbey gave us each a quarter for which we could spend on food to feed the animals, and this was all out of his own pocket. I remember one of the deer snuck up from behind and softly started munching an ice cream cone full of shelled corn that was in my hand. What fun!

On the way back while riding in his racy convertible, he let us sit on top of the back seat, with the wind blowing in our hair. (That was before all of the rules and regulations due to liability and litigation were implemented).That memory and many others are forever burned into my consciousness helping to form my character and adding to the foundation upon which to draw from as I journey through life.

Thank you so much, Mr. David! Abby!

~ Robert Feifar

2

The Principal and The Pie

I was a good kid. Only called to the principal's office once, and it was for handing out tiny Bibles to students when I was in elementary school. The principal was nice, so though it was a matter of correction from him, it wasn't traumatic. Still, the idea of getting called to the principal's office is scary.

Fast forward to middle school, where I made my very first lemon meringue pie in home economics class. I love lemon flavor, so I added a little extra lemon juice and extra lemon zest to the curd. It was the perfect tart-to-sweet ratio. In addition, I added just a touch of lemon zest to my meringue for extra flavor, and it held up just fine. The pie turned out great, and my cooking teacher was impressed, too.

The next morning, I brought a slice of the pie to my homeroom teacher because I liked him as a teacher. He said he would try it on his lunch break. I was excited to know his thoughts about it.

Imagine my surprise when I got called to the principal's office that afternoon. I didn't connect it to the pie, but when the principal asked if I was the one who gave a piece of lemon meringue pie to Mr. Smith, I gulped hard as I gave my answer.

Oh, no! Was it not okay to share? Was it wrong to give something to a teacher? All the anxieties and questions shouted at my brain, along with a healthy dose of guilt. I did nothing wrong on purpose. I hoped the principal would go easy on me.

Well, all my worries were for nothing. After confirming I was the baker who shared with the teacher, I braced for the principal's response. Rather than correcting me, the principal inquired about the remaining pie and requested a slice for himself. Um, that was not what I expected. He told me he was having lunch with my teacher who shared a bite with him. After tasting it, he decided it was the best lemon meringue pie he'd ever tasted.

Just wow! I can't recall if I gave him a slice that day or the next. However, I remember feeling encouraged about my cooking afterward. One class, two teachers, and one principal gave me the freedom to experiment with food all my life, and I still enjoy creating new flavors.

~ Crystal Murray

3

My First Piano Teacher

Miss Burbaugh was my first piano teacher. Since I was only six years old, she stipulated that I should also begin tap, ballet, gymnastics, and baton. Soon I was hip-hopping everywhere. Miss Burbaugh taught in our home while my parents were across the street at Dad's business.

So, it was always just the two of us in the house. I didn't mind unless she made me cry. Being so desperate for piano lessons it was decided later that I talked about her ruler and that she was being strict about the hand posture. She insisted I keep my fingers curved. She called it having "good soldiers." The ruler had been used to point to the notes on the page or tap the tempo, but it shocked me and hurt my hands when they were hit with it. All because I was not using curved fingers. Each time my hands were hit with the ruler I cried in shock and pain.

Miss Burbaugh would hug me tightly, and insist I become her "smiling little clown." I soon figured out the only way she was going to let me go from that hug was to stop crying and try my best to crack a smile; then the piano lesson would continue. After about three times of knuckle raps, I learned to maintain better hand positions. Even so, Miss Burbaugh was usually very pleasant and was thorough about teaching piano technique. Knowing she traveled into our small rural town to give lessons I was determined to keep the ruler incidents secret. She continued my lessons until we moved when I was 10, having just finished the fifth-grade.

While this was a different era of music education and some of Miss Burbaugh's methods may seem harsh, I learned several positive lessons which have served me well. I loved music and piano, so her lessons laid the foundation for my career. I continued studying piano wherever we lived and graduated college with a music teaching certificate, K through 12. I also realized my abilities in playing the pipe organ while in college. I began teaching piano and organ students of all ages and ability levels. I continued to use and teach the "good soldiers" hand position, but I never hit anyone's hands or made them cry.

Another positive result from the other four years of lessons I continued until we moved, is that I was able to teach my elementary school music classes dance and baton technique, which enhanced many of our bi-annual musical programs.

While stern, Miss Burbaugh provided her students with structure and lessons that reached beyond musical aptitude. I am certain we all benefitted from her intense devotion to her craft.

~ Charlotte Hunt Norris

4

Miss Miller

Miracle Worker in a Ponytail

Junior English was going to be a bore because the class before it was American History. The history teacher was a sub, pregnant, and so puffy and grouchy that all I remember about her was an owl-like pair of flat-lensed glasses and the fact that she left the room every ten minutes for the restroom.

We juniors were packed into an ancient dreary room of a four-room schoolhouse because our district was building onto the high school, and they didn't have a classroom big enough for all of us yet.

When the first-hour history teacher walked out of the room, cheery Miss Miller trotted in, and boredom left us.

It must have been her first year of teaching. She was petite, with an elf-like grin painted with glamorous red lipstick, a waist-length blonde ponytail, and that day a bright red skirt and red shoes. I think her ponytail hypnotized us. Everyone sat up, paid attention, and did whatever she told us to do. (Except for Wayne who decided he needed his cigarettes more and left the room as if he were pregnant, too.)

I learned from her because she made me believe in myself.

"Ask your parents what your name means. Ask your grandparents where your family came from. Ask, talk, invest your time, and listen to their stories. They will tell you who you are. Write it down. We'll talk about it in class."

I found out my grandfather could barely write English. He spoke English, but not very well. He learned English at the silent movies.

He wrote that my name meant "little horse"—that and another meaning he didn't want to tell me until I was grown up. Later I learned Holik meant "worthless."

I'm glad he waited because it was hard enough in high school then.

The day Miss Miller said we had to write a story for a final grade I didn't think I could do it. I wasn't feeling well. I took down the assignment and spent the next week with a bout of flu. About ten o'clock pm on the day before it was due I was still so sick I could barely focus on the page in front of me. I curled up in my bed and started writing. Finally, God woke my brain up just enough for me to fabricate a sad plot, and turn in a paper to our miracle worker, Miss Miller, who loved it and encouraged me to explore more through writing, which is now one avenue of my career.

~ Doris Holik Kelly

5

My Teacher, My Framework

Occasionally, we tend to reflect on the influences our teachers have had on our lives. Most of mine were good. My most influential teacher was Mrs. Laidley, head teacher, of the primary school I attended in rural St. Andrew, Jamaica. She came to my school in 1962, the year my country became independent.

On her first day, Mrs. Laidley posted a new chart, and I will never forget the words: 'For learning is better than silver or gold'. She thoroughly explained to us the meaning of independence. As the weeks went by, she ensured each child had a new school uniform and crepe soles to wear to the festivities in the city. I realized how much my teacher cared about each of us.

She engaged us in daily outdoor classes. Imagine being surrounded by pine trees, citrus trees, coffee shrubs, vegetables, and flowers. I always discovered something new and then I raced to write about it. When I asked my teacher for help, she often told me I should try to develop an independent mind. She praised my written work and said it was worthy of framing. Having noticed how much my love for writing had mushroomed, Mrs. Laidley said in order for me to write better, I needed to read more. I did and was confident when she asked me to assist the children who could not read well.

One morning, my frustration turned into amusement when Mrs. Laidley said I should pretend the disturbing noise from the river was the background music to my solo. In the end, she congratulated me and said my voice had also blended well with those of the John-to-wits and the Grassquits. (tropical birds)

Mrs. Laidley introduced technology into our school by acquiring a sewing machine, and at age ten I knew how to operate it. I loved my teacher, but one day she broke my heart. She encouraged my mother to send me to a school in the city where I would have a better opportunity to be successful in my entrance examination to begin my secondary education. It happened.

Although I have tried, I cannot recall the 'given name' of my inspirational teacher of five years who formed the framework of my life; the primary force behind my teaching and writing aspirations. Her adventurous classes helped me to develop an appreciation for nature. I will continue telling others to think independently and that learning is better than silver or gold.

~ Dorothy Purge

6

The Captivating Miss Mc

Teachers have always played an important role in my life. I vividly remember and can name every teacher I ever had, good and bad, but most importantly the good ones.

It will surprise most who now know me that I was a dreadfully timid and unassured kid. I recently found a box my old report cards proof of my school record. I was intrigued by the teachers' comments. Most confirmed my memories, stating I was a good, helpful and kind student, loved reading and science, made friends easily, and enjoyed informal group discussions, BUT was very reticent to speak in formal situations.

Going back in time, I clearly remember one traumatic day for me. Yet again another weekly book report assigned by my fourth-grade reading teacher. Mrs. Mamie Howard. She was delightful, positive, and made learning fun while challenging us. .

These were not run-of-the-mill reports. At her insistence, we shared the story from any character's point of view, except the protagonist, all while in costume. I, a lanky prepubescent girl, trembling, with rivulets of sweat running down my face, stood before the class in a costume pulled together from the cloakroom's footlocker. Charlotte's Web would never be as dramatic again.

The class erupted in laughter as I came center-stage. The taunts grew more raucous as I tried to be brave and speak as Charlotte, the spider in the story. My frail voice trailed off as I fled the classroom sobbing, with most of the boys heckling, "Ekk, a spider, stomp it!" and "Sooiee, let's eat Wilbur!" While we lived in a subdivision, many students had chickens and pigs at home, so they were familiar with animal life, but not me.

Mrs. Howard regained control and reprimanded the class, having them write apology letters to me. Additionally, she wisely and *strongly* recommended I be put in private speech classes. I thank her every day for introducing me to the most unorthodox woman I have ever known. The enchanting Miss Gertrude "Tut" McFarland, my deliciously rebellious speech teacher.

Miss Mc always dressed in glamorous and theatrical clothes and make-up. She captivated our attention, but her unyielding belief in her hodgepodge of misfit students' abilities made her mythical to many of us. At her insistence, we were not a lost cause. She challenged all her students to reach inside and find the voice we so longed to be heard, and use it. Always encouraging, yet demanding, she had us doing things many thought impossible for us… recitations, performing one-act plays and skits at school and PTA assemblies, and teacher meetings. I had to present dramatic and spirited short renditions of *The Song of Hiawatha* and *Paul Revere's Ride*.

I was able to visit Mrs. Mc several times as an adult and share my gratitude before she died at the age of 90. She was still acting and directing in community theater. Miss Mc was devoted to our little north Georgia slice of heaven; teaching public school until retirement age, serving on many local charitable boards, modeling the appreciation for diverse voices, respect, and integrity.

Even without her physical presence, Miss Mc still mentors me, fanning my passion for literature, storytelling, and teaching others, especially children. With it being imperative each learns that they are special and *can* learn. I want to pay forward the gift and legacy Gertrude McFarland has bestowed on me and many others.

Bravo, take another bow; and thank you, Miss. Mc.

~ Dara Armstrong Lehner

7

Watermelon Lips

A Teacher's Words Inspired a Little Heart

Her lips were redder than the inside of Daddy's summer watermelons. Ms. Middleton, my fourth-grade teacher, patted the top of my head with her chalky hand and said, "Do you think your parents would let me have you?" Her red lips spread across her face. "I think you're the best little girl I know."

Best little girl I know. I had never heard such words! Not a word tumbled out of my mouth. What could I say? Familiar words that tumbled from Daddy's alcohol breath were usually curse words.

"Lord help us." Mama often said. "I do not know when your daddy will come home from drinking. He lost his job and we'll be moving, again."

Did my fourth-grade teacher know how my heart hurt? Did she understand I had lost my best friend in the entire world when my cousin, Marylene, died in a car accident weeks before? Did Ms. Middleton see my shame each time Daddy staggered through the front door drunk? Did she care for me because of her tender compassion?

Had Ms. Middleton purposefully chosen her words to help a hurting child in need of encouragement? I ponder these questions. Ms. Middleton's words that flowed from her red watermelon lips became a memory that encouraged me throughout my childhood. Even in my adulthood, her words motivated me to press forward in tough times. Because of her example, I became a teacher, too! Today, her words still inspire me, especially when I see a slice of red, juicy watermelon.

~ Brenda Sue Bynum

8

Joe Tamillo

Only Your Best

You were the best coach a person could ever have. As a former Marine drill sergeant, you drilled and ran our cross-country team like an elite fighting force. It's one of the best things anyone ever did for me. You always demanded our best. You were hard on us, but we knew you cared more than we could even see at the time.

I can still hear you shouting, "Drive those knees, Lundell!" And "You can do it! Gut it out!"

One day after a meet I said, "Sorry, Coach. I could have run better." I expected a soothing, fatherly response like, "That's okay. Try again next week." But you didn't. You turned to me with piercing eyes and a terse, "Then why didn't you?" And without another word, you turned away again. I stood there speechless. End of conversation.

And that's what I needed—you who demanded my best, who accepted no excuses, who practiced very tough love.

We never made it to State, and we were all sorry for that. But you encouraged us when you said that what we had learned and how we had grown in character was more important than a state trophy and would carry us our entire lives. You were right. The integrity, the discipline, the guts to go beyond myself and not quit, and the honor of being one of your runners whom you took from boyhood to manhood—this and more have carried me my entire life. Because of you, I learned to be a marathoner in all things of life, to be disciplined, to see the long picture, to endure, to never give up before it's time to finish, and then to finish well.

As I write this I weep—as I wept every time I wrote and thanked you since those days. My father died when I was four, and you filled a big gap in my life.

You were also one of my English teachers, and you took the risk of teaching a class you called "Old-fashioned Grammar" to high school seniors even when the faculty thought no one would take it. Your class was full to overflowing because we all knew your value as a man.

We experienced solid, applicable education at its finest. What I learned from you there formed the foundation of everything that followed in my writing and editing career.

Though you've passed on from this life, your legacy continues in me. And I have striven to pass it on to others, even in this letter.

~ Peter Lundell

9

Mrs. Draper

Hard Lessons in Integrity

During my senior year of high school, I participated in DECA (Distributive Education Clubs of America), a work-study program designed for students interested in business. I enjoyed the idea of only having the morning for school, and the afternoon for working and earning real money.

The head of the DECA program, Mrs. Draper, was a beautiful, classy lady. She was professional, all business, with the reputation of expecting nothing less than perfection. My first work assignment was to work with an optometry office as a clerk, doing simple office tasks of typing (on an IBM Selectric typewriter) and filing patient records. Occasionally, I assisted the optometrist with note-taking on patient exams.

As a student worker, I understood the rule that I could work in the office only during business hours. Since I was the ripe age of 16 years old, I thought I was above the rule—after all, we know everything—and I went in one afternoon when the office was closed. I was going on a trip but didn't want to miss any hours (or pay). The optometry office was attached to another business establishment and shared a common entrance. Connivingly, I convinced the receptionist of the office that I had permission to come in and work although the office was closed.

The optometry office was empty and quiet, allowing me to get a lot of work done. I smugly left a note with my work hours on it and what I'd accomplished on the office manager's desk.

The next day, Mrs. Draper called me into her office. She was upset with my disobeying the school's rules and the workplace expectations of DECA student workers. While she disciplined me, it was obvious, she was controlling her anger. I was informed that the optometrist was furious and had terminated me immediately. I don't remember much from that disciplinary session, but I excused myself to run to the bathroom.

Behind the closed door of a bathroom stall, I sobbed and sobbed over my stupidity. I felt so much shame and remorse for my prideful, selfish actions and lying. I heard someone enter, and I stifled my loud sobs. Then I heard Mrs. Draper say tenderly, "Debbie, I know you are upset. You are a good student, and your employer has highly praised your work." She continued, "I'm releasing you to go home. We will talk more in the morning when you've had time to think about why you did what you did. I am positive you will learn from this."

And learn from this painful experience, I did.

The follow-up disciplinary plan was painful but necessary for my growth. Mrs. Draper expected me to go to the optometrist, apologize for my disobedience, and state what I did wrong. That was a difficult and humbling course of action to follow.

I remember Mrs. Draper's strong spirit of excellence in how she taught, modeled, and disciplined. I didn't deserve the kindness she showed me in the bathroom, yet I've never forgotten it. That day, I learned integrity far exceeds accomplishment.

~Debbie Jordan

10

Mr. Denio

Shorthand for Nothing but the Best

At sixteen, I entered my senior year of high school filled with excitement for what lay ahead. The duration was short-lived when, after three weeks, I fell seriously ill.

The excitement of returning to school quickly turned to depression. Would I ever get caught up and graduate? My sister and brother quit school when they were in tenth-grade. I was determined to get my high school diploma.

While attending my business law class, Mr. Denio inquired if anyone had any questions. I lacked the bravery to inquire about the thoughts within my heart. A brave girl asked, "I'm working hard but struggle to keep up with the law and other things. I'm behind but want to graduate. Do you have any suggestions? *How did she know my thoughts?*

The most outstanding teacher was Mr. Denio. His students loved him for his gentle and meek demeanor. He had the status of a married man with seventeen children. Yes, that's accurate, seventeen, and his wife was expecting again. Despite being made fun of behind his back, he nurtured a deep love and compassion for his students.

He explained what he imparts to his children. Expect to face numerous obstacles as you journey through life. How we handle challenges influences who we become and what we achieve. Embrace courage, and don't hesitate to seek help.

Ask for help. I was so shy my face turned red when anyone started talking to me or asking me a question. How could I ask for help?

After an "F" appeared on my report card in shorthand, I mustered up the courage to walk the long corridor to his office. My heart raced, and my legs, which held me up to run track, went limp. I sat on a chair outside his office. I didn't hear the door open. "Hello, Josephine. I wondered when you would come to see me." His warmth and commitment peeled back the layers of failure and depression in my life. We met weekly throughout my senior year, and to this day, his words and faith continue to impact my life.

When we had an assembly, they gave out awards. There was a sense of disbelief as they called my name. The "F" turned into an "A."

I will never forget the man who began my journey of belief in myself and the lives of many students at Linton High School in Schenectady, New York.

~ Jo Massaro

11

The Spelling Bee

The year was 1968. My classmate Dan and I had just been declared co-winners of the city spelling bee. After seeking the eyes of our parents, we both looked for the presence of the teacher who had led us to this moment.

Mrs. Mary Pryor was my favorite teacher and the one who had the most influence on me. She taught seventh- grade Language Arts and managed to inspire us, and more particularly me, to embrace what, with a lesser teacher, could have been a fairly uninspiring class. Mrs. Pryor was committed to giving her students an educational experience from which they could both learn and enjoy.

Going back to the spelling bee, she spent countless hours after school preparing the six of us who had qualified. She made that time, which could have been brutally boring for a group of seventh-graders, fun and interesting. She did so well that, out of approximately 100 students, two of hers, Dan and I, tied for first place.

Mrs. Pryor imbued in me a love for writing. We wrote short stories, poems, essays, haikus and more. Toward the end of the year, she showed us how to put together a "book" of our class's writings. She taught us how to lay it out and when we were done with that, she copied (mimeographed for those of you who know!) one for each of us. Many years later, I found that my mother had put mine aside in a box of things she saved for me.

Mrs. Pryor was truly an inspiration for me. She taught me, and many others, that learning can be exciting, interesting, and even fun! As a result, I have continued to learn throughout my life. Even now I am taking an online course. For that, I thank you, Mrs. Pryor!

~ Kathy Kuzas

The Landis Legacy

In the third-grade, I had a teacher who completely changed my outlook on school. Mrs. Landis was one of the kindest teachers I've ever met. She truly took the time to create a personal bond with each of her students and even keeps in touch with some of us to this day. Her active involvement changed me. Even from a young age, she taught me skills that would stick with me for a lifetime.

I feel one of the most valuable things Mrs. Landis taught me was how to be genuinely kind. I learned by example; even when she was upset you would never find her talking down or showing anger to someone. In fact, she would go out of her way to help anyone, even if she had been hurt by their actions or words.

She was thrilled at opportunities to teach us things extending the curriculum, particularly if we showed an interest in a subject that paralleled the lesson she was teaching. Mrs. Landis was a fabulous mentor as I advanced through school. She truly changed my whole outlook on learning. Even today, lessons I learned from her I use in my daily life.

Mrs. Landis provided so many opportunities which were student-centered. We all had to learn to respect others. One of my favorite activities was reading and she took that and ran with it. We would bring in our favorite books each week and would get to read them aloud to the class for story time. It was such a fun experience, we got to play teacher, unaware we were practicing our reading and public speaking skills; while mastering patience, respect, and listening skills.

She modeled ways we could be helpful. Mrs. Landis actively involved us in every aspect of her teaching when she could. She would walk us through grading another student's papers. She would talk us through lesson plans and let us talk to her about what we needed and wanted academically.

I vividly remember her acknowledging we were feeling cooped up inside a classroom; after all, we were third-graders. The Landis solution was to move the class outside and continue teaching as normal.

Mrs. Landis was always very patient and understanding, if we needed a break, we would get a minute to regain control. I carry a lot of what she taught me throughout my life today. As I homeschool my boys now, I keep her in mind while I'm preparing my school day with them. I know her legacy will continue through all who were privileged to have had her as a teacher.

~ Kayla Brocious

Capt'n K

So Say Us All, So Be It

High school years are a roller coaster for most teenagers as they traverse the minefield of academics, or lack of; young love and heartbreak, parties, proms, sports, first jobs, first cars, semi-independence, and career choices. My high school years were exciting, but at times exasperating.

I was quickly and continually forced to learn to be more adaptable and gregarious to survive my stint in multiple high schools in different states. Our dad's job promotions took our family from the town he was born and raised in and at that point where I had lived since I was four. We moved from the security of known surroundings and long-term friendships to the totally unknown and insecurity of everything in large metropolitan cities.

As I transferred my senior year, I thought I could glide through my senior classes. Unfortunately, I would not have enough credits to graduate unless I carried all academic courses, no "crip" classes for me. I also needed two science credits to meet the North Carolina graduation requirements. The principal secured permission from the Superintendent for me to double up on Chemistry, which they normally didn't offer.

I was quickly introduced to a class of fun, smart, high-achieving, and popular kids. No way I would fit in, I was the new kid in town and already behind in my studies. And then in walked in Mr. Earl Kirkland. He became my most challenging teacher to date. Capt'n. K, as he was known to his senior-only advanced Chemistry class, ran a tight ship. His insistence on excellence and his unfathomable belief I (we) would be a success still influence my ongoing teaching endeavors today.

I became Capt'n K's sole student in an independent study Chemistry class. This made up for the missing credit. It also gave him the chance to teach me more than just a Chemistry curriculum. He found out I had an interest in teaching and knew I was struggling to keep up with my other classmates , so I became his teaching assistant.

He would go over the lesson to make sure I understood it, then put me in front of the introductory Chemistry class to teach. Capt'n K never let me fail. If I made a mistake, he would continue to question me in front of the class. The questions guide my mind back to the correct information. I also set up labs, graded tests and homework which reinforced my senior class, while teaching me to think logically through the scientific process.

Chemistry became comfortable for me. Of course, he had a wonderful rapport with the Seniors, he used humor, but accepted nothing but excellence, particularly on his ten-page hand written mimeographed legal-sized homework assignments. His catchphrase, after we had looked over the homework or class notes, was always, "So say us all…so be it."

Many years laters, after I became a mother, and went back to college, one of my professors encouraged us to reconnect with an influential teacher. I chose Mr. Kirkland. He was thrilled to hear from me and told me how much he appreciated the contact. He made me promise to teach as he had taught me, to always challenge a student, to be there to guide them, but make them find the answer. I promised I would and that wewould stay in touch. It wasn't to be.

This dedicated and revered teacher died two weeks after we reconnected. I'm sure I am not the only student Capt'n K inspired. So say us all…so be it !

~ Dara Armstrong Lehner

14

Grammar Guru

A semicolon separates two complete thoughts."

"Subject and verb must agree."

"Eat that banana! Interjections are used at the end of an exclamation."

These lessons are just a few I learned under the tutelage of the "Grammar Guru," Robert Cox.

In the small town where I grew up, the middle and high schools were housed in the same building. My eighth-grade year, Robert, the junior/senior English teacher, was sent upstairs to teach my English class, and he immediately recognized my writing talent and appointed me as the middle school correspondent for the high school newspaper, which he sponsored. That started an extensive mentor-student relationship.

When I moved into high school the next year, I majored in the "Robert Cox" curriculum: Journalism for four years, Junior English, and Senior Honors English. We didn't stop there: he also taught my first two college English classes.

I have co-authored a traditionally published book and contributed to several others, and I attribute much of that success to Robert's rigorous instruction in punctuation, grammar, and writing in general. He left no stone unturned, and no comma mistake unmarked. I sometimes thought he was too tough on me and my fellow classmates, but, when I followed in his footsteps and became a teacher myself, I realized he wanted his students to succeed, as I do.

It was not all serious business in his classes; Robert used his sly sense of humor effectively to illustrate different points. He made learning fun, which I have tried to emulate in my classroom.

My relationship with Rob—it took me years to keep from calling him "Mr. Cox"—continued when I left his classroom over 40 years ago. I have served as a babysitter for his children; we have traveled together to different places; he was the Best Man in my wedding. Beyond the discussion of commas, periods, and subject/verb agreement, we have maintained a long friendship with enough in-jokes to fill several volumes.

Rob recently joined my graduating class for a reunion, and he seemed to have more fun than any of my classmates. During a tour of our old school, he was ecstatic when he found the podium he had used in our classroom. Though he is now enjoying the retired life, his legacy lives on in former students like me who still utilize his lessons in our everyday lives.

Now, use that interjection and eat that banana!

~ Carlton Hughes

15

Mentors

Have you ever stopped to realize how gifted you are? Have you looked back at your life and recalled the people who came alongside you and guided you onto a positive path? Have you taken inventory of your abilities and reflected on how you arrived at this point?

I did, and this is what I discovered. Being born during the Great Depression, money was extremely scarce, and few people could afford doctor's visits. Yet, my mother worried about me as I didn't talk until I was three. Years later a doctor diagnosed me with dyslexia thus explaining why speaking, especially in school, had been so difficult.

A quiet student doesn't come near defining my behavior. Timid would be a better word. It all changed when Mr. Henderson came into my life. The dean of girls in my high school encouraged me to sign up for his public speaking class starting my junior year. The class consisted mainly of football players seeking an "easy grade." But for me, it was a game changer.

Standing in front of the class reading my assignments proved extremely painful. The boys whistled and giggled, and when I finished, they would applaud like crazy. My face flushed, turning five shades of red as embarrassment washed over me. Mr. Henderson, our instructor, was also an amazing person who encouraged me to continue when I suggested that the class wasn't for me.

"Give it a little more time," he suggested. "See these unruly boys as your cheerleaders. You need to realize your audience all get out of bed sleepy-eyed and disheveled just like you," he'd laugh.

He did his best to control the boys, and over the year he taught me many tricks speakers use to curb anxiety. He loved teaching and his gentle ways proved it.

With his unlimited patience and skillful guidance, I received an A for the class, and eventually used much of what he taught me when I became a public speaker. I wrote him an encouraging letter explaining how he changed my life and thanked him repeatedly. I celebrate Mr. Henderson and teachers like him who go the extra mile to inspire and enlighten their students. God bless them all.

~ Bette Lafferty

Grateful For It All!

At the lowest point of my life, October 17, 1986, 39 years old, ten days earlier my drug-addicted, abusive, second husband of only two years, ripped off my shirt outside, facing the street, in front of my three young children. I was taking them to school that morning. I ran into the house frightened, not knowing what would come next. My children, seven, nine, and ten years old, running behind me. My husband enraged, threw me on the floor, grabbed me by the neck, and began choking me. I could hear my children, screaming and crying, Mommy, Mommy! I began to lose consciousness. Then he let go.

A mother of the church paid for one-way tickets to fly me and my children back home to Wilson, NC. I was ashamed, broken, and disgusted with myself. I lived in fear that my husband would soon discover I was in Wilson and come after me.

Two weeks after arriving back home, I took my children to my family's home church. On that fateful Sunday, I met the woman who would change the course of my life and the lives of thousands of marginalized children and families forever, Sallie Baldwin Howard.

Sallie was the head of Christian Education. I placed my children in that department and volunteered to work with her. I became her protégé. She invited me to her home and shared her extensive knowledge and library of ancient African and African American history. Books like, "They Came Before Columbus", and the Nile Valley Conference tapes.

I had never heard or read about the story of our Ancient African heritage. That knowledge took root in me and transformed how I saw myself and the people to whom I belong. I began to see myself as a proud descendant of the great Ancient Africans. In the lineage of the people who gave the world its first stone buildings, who lifted the pyramids above the Nile, who gave the world its first alphabet, and who taught the world to read and write. I was on fire for everything she shared with me. I fully embraced Sallie's vision and mission as my own.

Moreover, I dedicated myself to making sure that every child we served at the YEP (Youth Enrichment Program) summer program and Sallie B. Howard School and that I founded would come to know and believe for themselves that "You are somebody. Your circumstances don't determine who you shall be or what you can accomplish. You can be more than you ever thought you could become."

~ JoAnne Coble Woodard, PhD

My Favorite Teachers

Who were my favorite, unforgettable teachers growing up? Well Mrs Pratt in second-grade comes first to mind. She and I got along well after my parents explained to her my first name was not Jessie but Jessie Lee. She was upset at me for not responding to Jessie. You see, I was named for my paternal grandmother, Jessie Lee Nixon. Over time people shortened her name to just "Jessie". When I came along, it had been decided to call me Jessie Lee. When I heard Jessie, I thought you were talking to my grandmother. So, I ignored you!

The next teacher I really liked was Miss Duke in fourth-grade. She would read to us a chapter after lunch. One book she read was, The Lion, The Witch, and the Wardrobe by C. S. Lewis. I fell in love with C.S Lewis and the Narnia Tales, because of her! She was also very musically oriented. She played the autoharp and would lead us in songs, at least once a week, usually right before time to go home.

Next came Mr. Bruce in seventh-grade. Mr. Bruce was very different from any other teacher I ever had at any time in my schooling. He loved to challenge students. His area was Science and he was my homeroom teacher for seventh-grade. He started each morning in the classroom, eating breakfast of plain yogurt, honey, and a tablespoon of vinegar. Why? His response was it helped his digestion.

We had a large fish tank in our homeroom that contained a red-bellied piranha. The kids in my class really got a kick out of this predator. We fed it goldfish. The only problem we encountered was it would come after fingers if you tried to pick something out of the tank. And we had to keep the tank from getting too cold or freezing.

We had steam heat in our classroom and sometimes on Mondays we would come in to see a very sluggish, hardly moving fish. It was a real challenge to try and warm up the tank and get the piranha swimming again. We learned a bunch about life and science from Mr Bruce.

The last two teachers I would like to discuss are Mr. Robert Peterson and Mr. Peter J Hargis. Both were high school music teachers, and both taught me something about myself. Mr. Peterson encouraged me to sing, that I had a good voice and even let me do a solo during our Christmas Cantata as a freshman. He also introduced me to Madrigals, 15th & 16th century songs sung by a small group of singers. These had different parts you had to pay attention to as you sang. I really loved these songs! Mr. Hargis was my music teacher from tenth through twelfth grade. I was part of a select choral group called Choraliers. This group sang as part of the school chorus but also did concerts on our own. We sang everywhere, nursing homes, Disney, school, music contests. I also learned to ring handbells and continued singing Madrigals. Here I learned I loved to sing but really wanted to keep that part of me as a hobby not concentrate on music as a profession. To this day I love to sing with the radio or CD, etc.

All of these teachers touched me in some way or fashion, helping guide me along. Sometimes God puts people in our sphere to challenge or get us to see things we would not see otherwise. Sometimes with a nudge, sometimes with a completely different viewpoint.

~ Jessie L Collins

18

Mr. Carl Simpson
An Angel in Teacher's Clothing

When thinking back on my journey through school, two teachers helped to mold, encourage, and inspire me. That's right, not just one, but two! And you know what? They were both men. There's too much to say about both of them for just one essay, so in this writing, I am going to tell you about just one of them.

In my high school years, Mr. Carl Simpson shines above all the teachers I have had. Not to say there weren't other good teachers, but for me, Mr. Simpson tops them all.

I had the pleasure of having Mr. Simpson for three classes in high school: Theater of Arts, Psychology, and Journalism. He was gifted in the fact he got down on our level as teenagers, without sacrificing a bit of the integrity and leadership qualities that make a great teacher.

In Theater of Arts class, for instance, Mr. Simpson coached us on the best way to get into, and literally become the character we were trying to portray. His gifting and creativity made it easy to model exactly how to fit yourself into the character you were depicting.

For Psychology class Mr. Simpson would teach us from the required readings of the psych class, of course, while also bringing fun into our learning experience. As an example, Mr. Simpson was adept at hypnosis. You heard right, HYPNOSIS!

Upon first hearing about it, I'm sure that our parents were horrified. But take it from me, looking back it was anything but dangerous. One time he hypnotized one of my friends, *(we'll call him Paul)*, and told him when he woke up he would not be able to put his arm down. When Paul woke up he didn't immediately realize he couldn't put his arm down. And when he noticed his arm was up, he was bewildered as to why he could not put it down. The whole class got a big laugh out of it.

Of course, Mr. Simpson reversed the hypnotic suggestion and Paul never had that problem again.

The third class I had with Mr. Simpson was Journalism, and we were in charge of putting out the school newspaper each month. Our class nominated and voted on officers for the paper and to my surprise, I was voted in as the editor. As a result, operating as the editor of the school newspaper that semester served to build character, enhance my self-esteem, and gave me confidence in my ability to write better.

Needless to say, these memories and more were burned into my consciousness, and have helped to forever mold me in life's journey. Thank you so much, Mr. Carl Simpson!

~ Robert Feifar

19

Two Divine Encouragers

What could a high school English teacher and Home Economics teacher have in common?

Each one impacted my life and my future.

In a small east Texas town, Mr. Clinton, a recent college graduate, taught English, and wanted me to become an English teacher. His excitement about the subject transferred to his students, and especially to me as he gave us opportunities for creative writing.

Jewell Hunter, the Home Economics teacher, taught the young ladies how to sew and cook. She was so patient with us, and we loved her for it. Mrs. Hunter demanded our best and we worked diligently on our projects.

In my senior year, we girls took the Betty Crocker Homemaker of Tomorrow written exam sponsored by General Mills. Winners of each state were given a college scholarship plus a trip to Washington, DC and Williamsburg, VA. I was amazed to win for the state of Texas. I had always wanted to become a nurse, but I didn't know how my family could afford college tuition. Because of Mrs. Hunter, I received a B.S. degree in nursing from Texas Woman's University. Shortly after graduation, I married Dr. Jim Sandin, the love of my life.

Fast forward. My husband and I started our family following his tour of duty as a medical officer in Vietnam. We were blessed with Steve, Angie, and Jeffrey. Sadly, our seventeen-month-old, Jeffrey, died suddenly of bacterial meningitis. I was devastated. As a believer in Jesus Christ, I had many questions but couldn't find a book with answers. Over a period of years, I felt the Lord leading me to write a book, helping other grieving parents. Through many tears, Bible study, and prayers, I wrote *See You Later, Jeffrey,* and saw it in print with Tyndale after eleven years and on the twenty-seventh submission. That is how my writing career began, thanks to the influence of Mr. Clinton.

About five years after the book was published, my husband and I visited Mr. Clinton in another state, and I gave him an autographed copy of the book and expressed my appreciation for his encouragement. It meant so much to me to have that opportunity to say, "Thank you."

Now you can understand how these two wonderful teachers influenced my life. To God be the Glory!

~ Fran Caffey Sandin

20

I Was Heard

All through high school, I was never in the popular crowd. I was always in the background, ready to participate if asked. I was the girl in the back of the room standing quietly in the corner, head down, not speaking with anyone. The girl who was laughed at, called names ("hey fatty"), who wanted to "fit in" but never could…never allowed.

When I went to college, nothing changed. I was rarely invited to participate in any activities, no matter where they were or who was involved.

Yet one professor saw something in me, saw me for who I was and who I was meant to become. She showed me I was someone. I was smart. I had a voice. I was heard. She was my Oral Interpretation professor, Dr. Sheron Dailey. Because of her, I grew into a confident person. Not afraid of showing me for me. She encouraged me to step up and step out. To stand tall. To show the world what I can do. Because of her, I dared to participate, to get involved. I was chosen to compete in different performance contests, as a solo, as a duet, and as a group, competing and winning.

Even after I graduated from college, Dr. D was there for me. We kept in touch, sending cards and notes to each other. When I was working on my PhD and having difficulties, she was there. She supported me through many tough decisions concerning my degree. She was there when I needed someone "who had been there before" to listen, to understand.

I am truly grateful for everything she has given me—her support, her shoulder, her time—but most importantly, her friendship.

~ Kim Autrey

~ Kim Autrey

21

Mr. Anderson

YSCYMTM

Mr. Anderson was the most sought-after teacher at the rural community college I attended in Ohio. His reputation was bordering on legendary for his feats of prowess in teaching his anxiety-blocked students the magic of math.

I knew of him for a few semesters before I was fortunate enough to become one of his forever grateful students. That first day in his class was the beginning of my future success as a student, and much later, as a teacher. He became my standard of excellence as he took his students from ignorance and frustration with math to just skill and confidence.

Mr. Anderson has the intelligence and the knowledge to teach upper-level math. Yet, he chose to instruct the struggling students who could not overcome their former failures in this formidable subject. That kind of commitment to others is rare.

Every day this unassuming professor who had co-authored textbooks made himself available and understandable to his students. He broke down complex concepts into a steady, logical foundation of knowledge and understanding previously unknown to his students.

He had liberal office hours, devoting many hours of his personal time to each one of his students. The poster on his office door is etched into my memory. It showed a young man clutching his head in pain as he worked on a difficult math problem. This showed how much Mr. Anderson truly understood his students' struggles. He would patiently, kindly lead us through our misunderstandings and our mistakes with grace.

Mr. Anderson was passionate about the scope and beauty of mathematics. He loved its precision and its methodology in reducing complex problems into sound solutions. But more than that, he was passionate about making this beauty and precision attainable for his students. He simply didn't want us to earn good grades and pass tests. He wanted us to grasp the deeper concepts that went far beyond those temporary goals. He also enabled his students to translate those mathematical principles to life situations.

Celebrating his students' successes was a joy for Mr. Anderson and his students. I will always remember the day I received his highest praise in the form of an acronym - YSCYMTM emblazoned on the top of a unit test paper. I smiled at the irony of this code for what it stood for "You Should Change Your Major To Math

~Ann Tantlinger

22

Tribute to Mervin Chang

of Cabrillo High School, Lompoc, California

I should confess that I wasn't an A-student in high school. I was too distracted by sports, girls, and the glorious sunshine of Southern California, where it never rains. Okay, it rains occasionally. And that's about how often my imagination was captured by a teacher. That was not their fault, but mine.

But for reasons I still can't explain, my imagination was captured by a new teacher at Cabrillo High School, Lompoc, California, Mervin Chang. It wasn't that he was cool that drew me into his teaching, although he was plenty cool. He was from Hawaii, helped coach wrestling, liked to surf, and even brought cooked snails to class one day. I'd have called them escargot, but that wasn't in my vocabulary at the time.

He taught old-school drafting and graphic arts in the mid-1970s. Even though I wasn't a great student, I thought I wanted to be an engineer, so I signed up to take all his drafting classes. These were the days of lead pencils, T-squares, plastic triangles, and templates, very unlike working with today's cad-cam computer programs. We spent hours on hard stools hunched over a drafting table scribing mechanical drawings of gears and screws or architectural drawings of businesses or homes. We painted elevations and made models of our designs. I must have had four of his classes during my high school career.

Mr. Chang was an amazing teacher with very high expectations of his students. He was also an artist. He taught me to be concerned about lines and angles and where they met one another. Precision was a key to good design and drawing. He could also pen the most glorious calligraphy and was often invited by the school to add names to diplomas and awards. He never taught me calligraphy but because of my admiration for him and his gifts, I picked it up on the side. I still use those skills today, some fifty-odd years later.

But beyond his instructional skills and his own artistry, what captured me most was that he took an interest in me and my future. I could tell he wanted me to succeed, and his classroom demeanor was evidence that he actually cared. He didn't try to be a buddy, but he was a very generous mentor, always willing to help students go beyond what they thought they were capable of. He inspired me to do my best work in his class. I wanted to measure up to those high expectations of Mervin Chang. I wanted to be like him in all the ways I could.

After graduating from high school, I moved from the flower capital of the world to the carpet capital of the world, Dalton, Georgia. I planned to go back to California at the end of the summer to play junior college football. I didn't. I ended up staying. In part, it was because I spotted an advertisement in the local newspaper of a company looking for a draftsman. I didn't think I had a snowball's chance of getting that kind of job right out of high school, but because in the interview process, it became evident to the employer that I knew my stuff, I got to job and life unfolded.

I don't know what ever happened to Mr. Chang. I know he continued to teach at Cabrillo High School for some years after I graduated, but I will always be in his debt. Although I had several drafting jobs and even a semester of college-level engineering, I didn't remain a draftsman. In fact, I ended up doing degrees in theology and philosophy, about as far away from mechanical drawing as one could get. But I ended up teaching in a classroom for over 30 years. I still use my drafting and lettering skills. More importantly, I have tried to be the kind of inspiring teacher and mentor to others that Mervin Chang was to me. Thank you, Mervin Chang!

~ C. Ben Mitchell, PhD

23

Diagramming Dilemma

Learning was always an adventure for me. Every fall I looked forward to going back to school even though I was nervous about what the new teacher would be requiring of us. However, diagramming sentences in middle school was not exactly my favorite pastime. School House Rock had not arrived on TV yet and I had no idea where Conjunction Junction was located on the map. But Mrs. Kepler was dogmatic in trying to keep us eighth-graders on track with adverbs, adjectives, simple and compound sentences, proper punctuation, and no hanging participles.

There seemed to be an abundance of students who were apt to use local colloquialisms in our daily speech. Warsh, 'rench and ain't were just plain common talk to many of us. And then there were those of us who knew what was expected and used them anyway - just to be ornery. Mrs. K was always trying to correct us and turn us into more sophisticated humans. Of course, it didn't help when she became our junior-year English literature and grammar instructor. We knew better but tried our best to convince her to allow at least the word ain't. But she stuck to her guns and we continued diagramming and punctuation drills.

Two years later I sat in English 101 at university and imagine my surprise when I found the class diagramming sentences all over again!

Be proud Mrs. K - it was the only class I earned an A in that semester and it felt like a breeze.

Mrs. Sarah Kepler, you succeeded with at least one of us. And yes, I do wash and rinse the dishes! That ain't no lie.

~ Robert Ousnamer

24

The Guiding Lights

Teachers Who Inspired My Journey Into Education

As I think back on my journey to my career in education, I am reminded of the impact certain teachers had on shaping my path. These teachers were beacons of inspiration, as they guided me with their belief in my potential, their high standards, and their non-stop encouragement.

One such teacher was Mrs. Hines, my high school English teacher. With her dynamic teaching style and passion for literature, she developed a deep appreciation for the literature. Missus Hines never settled for anything but our best, she challenged our thinking and pushed our thinking beyond our limits. She created an environment where our best was always expected. She helped me overcome my writers block by telling me personal stories about her struggles. She made me see that what I was struggling with was some something I could overcome.

Another influential figure was Miss Lee, my math teacher. I was always great at seeing math concepts after I saw patterns. Miss Lee spent countless hours after school helping me understand math. She never once doubted I would be successful. Miss Lee also made our class fun. She challenged us with real life math equations and encouraged us to find math problems in our lives to bring to class. Miss Lee's unwavering support taught me that failure is not the end but a step to growth. I use this in my career as a teacher . I never let my students give up on themselves.

These teachers, with their dedication and passion developed the love of teaching in me. They carved a path that led me to pursue a career in education. Their belief in me even when I had doubts, constantly reminded me of the power of a teacher. Inspired by their example, I will pay forward the lessons they taught me, hoping to empower and inspire the next generation of students to be all that they can be.

~ Viloshinee "Vee" Murugan

over too soon, but I went on to write a three-book series about the Historic Triangle of Mackinac.

I got an A, and as I laughed in relief, Doc's reaction was: "My wife and I are going away this weekend. To Mackinac Island! You have encouraged me to expand my horizons." He said I had a gift for describing and crafting voices that made people listen.

Thank you, Doc., I'm still writing. I just had book number five published.

~ Doris Holik Kelly

26

Mr Witt

Blind Inspiration

I knew him as Mr. Witt. He was my last piano teacher before leaving for college in Bethany, West Virginia. I had never been interviewed or auditioned to be accepted as a piano student before that day.

The piano teacher I had previously was moving and recommended him. She told me he was the best for me. I was 14 years old when I walked into Mr. Witt's home, with my music book books in hand. When his wife introduced us, his blindness became real to me. He couldn't see anything! How was this going to work?

My mother and I followed him into the music room, where chairs and a baby grand piano awaited us. Mr. Witt explained he lost his eyesight at the age of 33 because of diabetes. He showed me his music books in Braille, you can't read Braille music notes, and play at the same time! But I didn't talk about it. I didn't know what to say, I had never been interviewed.

And so, the audition began as I began playing his piano. I felt at ease because my mother sat behind me in the music room. Then Mr. Witt explained he was going to come behind me while I played and put his hands on my hands. He was checking my hand posture. My mother nodded to say he approved, for he smiled and sat back in his chair. Thank you Mrs Burbaugh, my first piano teacher, who insisted on good hand posture.

I had four piano teachers before Mr. Witt because of Dad's promotions in his job. Each one taught me well, but no one addressed how to bring out the melody louder than other notes. It meant adding weight to the fingers playing the melody.

I remember while playing a 16th note run in a classic Chopin piece, Mr. Witt stopped me. He recommended I change the finger I was using to play a certain note. When I asked why, he revealed the weight used to play that one note was wrong. What an ear!

Mr. Witt also taught special pedal techniques for expression. Decades later I'm often complimented on the expression I put into my piano music. I will always remember your kindness and interest in my success. I remember… Thank you, Mt. Witt!

~ Charlotte Hunt Norris

27

Teachers Make a Difference

"Back in the day", this would have been 1953…I think. It was seventh-grade, I remember that for sure. My home had never been stable. Some days we would play board games, clean the house, have some laughs, and remember family that lived in another part of the state. Dad had moved to Fayetteville, North Carolina for a job, so there were no relatives around here. On other days it could be hard to deal with, unhappy parents, with lots of disappointments in their lives. These disappointments rolled over onto their parenting skills and I wasn't given a lot of "atta boys".

I heard the word stupid more than not most days, which rubbed off on a 13-year-old with a narrow vision of life. There were music lessons, which were dropped due to lack of funds almost as soon as they started. There were movies attended, that showed lots of show tunes with talented stars, but no outlets for dreams or visions of what "might be". No encouragement to dream, imagine what could be, or where one might aspire to something better. I wasn't smart enough to make life any different than what was in front of me, which was the poor part of town with little hope.

My grades were at the bottom of the barrel. Not because I tried and failed, but because I didn't try and failed. I had no interest in grades, school, or teachers, except for the boys. Not that I knew what to do with boys, but in looking for acceptance and acknowledgment of "seeing me", I longed for appreciation. Anybody that paid attention to me received my attention.

There were far and few in seventh-grade, so mostly I kept company with other 13-year-old girls who were in the same boat. Not knowing education was the key to a better way of life. Not expecting life to be much different than the situations we found ourselves in daily. Our conversations and energies were directed to movies and boys. And seeing the "well to do" with all the fun activities we couldn't aspire to attend, i.e. ball games, dances, and clubs. So, some envy of what "if we had" … While believing the language that came from our parents that we were not up to doing anything well and didn't have smarts.

In the seventh-grade you had the test, (which I think evolved into the SAT over the years), which told something of your ability. My teacher called me over for a private word after the scores were made available to her. This lady informed me I was smart. That I had scored well above average, and my work and grades were not reflecting this score.

What? I was smart? I was amazed and carry that conversation to this day. What a difference it made, in my self-confidence.

The conversation made a total difference in my approach to my attitude towards other seventh-graders and years down the road, I started making decisions that took thought. The thoughts I had never used, thought about, or felt I could use.

I'm sorry to say I failed to increase my grades for many more years of school. I didn't step into many a "stupid" situation that I would have followed without question before this lady revealed my "smarts". I still made some stupid decisions but in my immaturity, I didn't have enough knowledge not to.

In later years, I realized this was not something she was to reveal to a student. A parent, yes, but not a student. But this student appreciated it and still does to this day. It made a difference in my approach to every job I held, it made a difference in my grades when I finally matured into adulthood and started paying for my own school. It made a difference in my relationship with men and people in general.

The self-worth it gave me was invaluable. The intimidation I felt for anyone who seemed to be in a better place was reduced to a normal appreciation. Not the concern, I could never have, do, be there. I had the smarts, I had to choose to do it. I was capable, just had to want it.

I have blessed this lady for years, for giving me a step out of a self-defeating attitude.

~ Tonie Neal

28

The Teacher, The Guide, and The Encourager

I loved school. From day one in kindergarten until the day I walked across the stage to receive my high school diploma, I enjoyed everything about school. Especially my teachers.

I had some really great teachers and some who left lasting impressions on me. But there was one teacher in high school who made more of an impact on my life than most of the others... Barbara Tripp, my biology teacher at Olympic High School in Charlotte NC.

Mrs. Tripp was a teacher who captured the attention of her students the minute we walked into her class. She brought the subject matter to life and we learned so much from her.

But this teacher was much more than just a teacher. She was a great guide for each of us. Mrs. Trippp has a passion for listening to us, and for learning about each of us as individuals. High school wasn't always easy, and having someone you can trust and confide in is important to anyone... but especially for teenagers. She learned about our families, our likes and dislikes, and took an interest in our dreams and ambitions. I always loved having my parents meet with her on parent-teacher nights because my parents were able to see how special she was.

Mrs. Tripp paid attention to my hopes of pursuing a degree in biology and delighted with that! She gave me great advice on my education beyond high school and encouraged me to reach for my dreams. She also encouraged me to become involved with the first Ecology club at our school which made such an impact on me; learning about the importance of taking care of our surroundings and planet. It was a fun experience learning from her, and I always made the effort to go back and visit her when I came home from college.

While I ended up changing my major at UNC-Chapel Hill, Mrs. Trippp was excited to hear about everything I was doing and learning in college... and making sure my heart was happy. She always made time to talk with me whenever I came home.

Mrs. Tripp holds a special place in my heart, and I owe her many things for all she has taught me, all of the good advice and guidance she shared with me, and for always encouraging me in all of my life endeavors. The best lessons from this wonderful teacher were about teaching with knowledge and excitement, taking an interest for those around us in kind and caring ways and to always, always offer encouragement to those around us.

My thanks to Mrs. Tripp for being a life teacher, guide, and encourager to me. They are the best life lessons I learned from one of the best teachers I had the privilege of learning from.

~ Joyce Dalgleish

29

Perspective

As I sit and think about the many teachers I have had in my life, there are many things I can say about them; some things good and some bad. However; when I think about the greatest instructor I have had, the name Reverend H. Maurice Barnes is always at the top.

I met Reverend Barnes at Shaw University when I was a sophomore in college. I was not a religion major but I always had a natural interest and curiosity about the Bible (Word of God), so I took as many religion classes as I could as electives. Throughout my life, I was subjected to some practices that did not seem quite right to me. At the time, I was not sure how I knew they were not right, but I was just uneasy with some religious practices.

Therefore; becoming a part of the class "Introduction to the Bible" was exactly what I needed. Reverend Barnes knew the Word of God and he was very confident in teaching it. He allowed us as students to grow in our thinking and explore subjects in the Bible that may have been controversial. He was skilled enough and knowledgeable enough to show the students how to look at the same scripture in different ways.

This learning process used by Reverend Barnes pushed the students to grow deeper in their relationship with God through the exegetical study of the scriptures and debating our findings with other students. By the time I completed this class, I learned how to interpret the Word of God, I had grown exponentially in my relationship with God and my peers and I was confident in my ability to carry the Word of God. I went on to take several other classes under Reverend Barnes and came to respect him as my professor, but also as a real man of God who exemplified the teachings of Christ in everything he said and did.

I learned to walk out the Scripture verse 2 Timothy 2:15 (KJV), "Study to shew thyself approved unto God, a workman that needeth not to be ashamed, rightly dividing the word of truth.".

God Bless you, Reverend H. Maurice Barnes, you are the consummate educator and a man after God's own heart.

Your Former Student

~ Melissa Grimes

30

Standards Of Excellence

My tenth-grade English teacher, Mr. Hunter, was my favorite in school. He presented a no-nonsense demeanor but was always professional and respectful, expecting nothing less from his colleagues or students.

Mr. Hunter refused to accept students' disrespectful or taunting comments of one another. It was his way, and his rules without question. If you tried to defy them, you were removed and sent to detention. This authority made students feel safe and secure enough to make mistakes. We never felt embarrassed or humiliated when he corrected us, and he shut down any derogatory comments anyone dared to attempt.

Although strict, I found Mr. Hunter exhibited compassion, patience, and understanding. He refused to accept less-than-quality work, requiring us to struggle with the idea of doing our best. He understood his students' abilities and would push us to do better, accepting nothing less than an 80.

I didn't always appreciate his demands. He expected all of us to give 100% to our work. A lesson I didn't appreciate. He wasn't just teaching for his class, he laid the foundation for excellence in other classes and our life.

One assignment exiplfies this concept. I remember having to write a paper three times. The first time I wrote it, I thought it was excellent. I had followed all the instructions, it was perfect….in my mind. I turned it in knowing I had done a phenomenal job and would exceed the minimum grade of 80. NOT!

When Mr. Hunter returned the papers in class, he dropped mine on my desk with a big F circled in red on top of the page. The comments on the paper read,, "This paper has no substance, and you did not go into depth. Re-do and turn it in tomorrow." I was flabbergasted! Not only did I have to do it over, but I had to complete all of my assignments for his and other classes in one night.

Excuses were out of the question. Mr. Hunter would never accept them, nor would my mother, a schoolteacher. I didn't want to entertain her disappointment or discipline if she found out. So I stayed up well past my bedtime, re-writing it with less confidence. That F was glaring at me. The next day, I handed my paper back, hoping to exceed everyone's expectations.

No news is good news, right? I waited a week before Mr Hunter returned my paper. This time I received a D, equivalent to a 60. I was devastated and cried. He wrote, "Do over, go further into depth, and return tomorrow." I was so angry and had visions of lashing out and screaming, "What's wrong with you, the world doesn't revolve around you! Do it yourself!"

The reality of another sleep-deprived night set in as I prayed for God's help to finish the paper and make Mr. Hunter happy. I took my time, I wrote, erased, crossed out, and tossed sheets in the trash. I read my paper over and over, asking myself if this was the last rewrite or if I would have to do it again. Finally finished, I turned it in.

The following day Mr. Hunter asked me to stay after class. Nervously, with sweaty palms, and a pounding heart I sat across from him as he took my paper from his desk and wrote 85 on it.

Before he could say a word, I jumped up, gave him the biggest hug, danced, and screamed. This was a shock to both of us. I was so stunned and overjoyed, I couldn't settle down. He said, "Barbara, get yourself together". Those words echoed in my mind then and now. I knew he was proud of me.

Today I still remember the pride I felt for struggling and succeeding. No one will ever say I can't write a paper, or succeed.

That day, Mr. Hunter, whom I admired, gave me a hard-earned grade of 85. I met his standards of excellence, and now they are mine.

~ Barbara Wright

Contributing Authors

Kim Autrey

Kim, a former composition instructor, works with authors helping them get their stories and voices out into the world. She is a proud wife and fur mom. When not helping others, she enjoys reading and being with family.

Kayla Brocious

Kayla Brocious is an energetic and enthusiastic young woman. She and her husband Derek are the parents of two sons, and are expecting their third son in the Fall. She homeschools the boys and they love to got out and explore nature and their community.

Brenda S. Bynum

Brenda Sue Bynum, author of children's books, is a writer who loves to bring childhood experiences that taught life lessons into her books. All her books were inspired by humble heroes impacting her life with the light of God's love.

Jessie L Collins

Jessie Collins is a retired nurse, editor, and formatter for a partnership publishing company. She enjoys many hobbies and lives in Central Florida with her husband. They are enjoying retirement.

Joyce L. Dalgleish

Joyce grew up in Charlotte, NC.and attended the University of North Carolina at Chapel Hill, earning a BA in Recreation Administration. After graduation, she began working in Human Resources at UNC, while also working part-time for the Durham Parks and Recreation Department for 15 years. Joyce also served as a volunteer youth leader and Sunday school teacher for over 31 years. In 2023, Joyce retired from UNC after 46 years in HR. She currently lives in the NC Triangle area with her fur babies.

Robert Feifar

Robert Feifar is a Christian. He is self-employed and the owner of a recording studio, Feifar Productions. He is a narrator, voice-over actor/artist, and does audio production. Bob likes to take prayer walks. He lives near Lake Michigan with his wife, Kelly. They have four grown children.

Melissa Grimes

Melissa B Grimes has served in education for more than 30 years as a principal, assistant principal, and currently, as a middle school English language arts teacher. She is married, has three children, and several grandchildren Melissa is a minister with her husband. She holds bachelors, masters, and doctorate degrees from four colleges and universities.

Carlton Hughes

Carlton Hughes wears many hats. He is a professor of communication, a children's pastor, and a freelance writer whose work has been featured in many prominent periodicals and devotional books. He recently coauthored *Adventures in Fatherhood*. Carlton is an empty-nesting dad and devoted husband who enjoys classic sitcoms, all chocolate and enjoys dressing up as crazy characters and making videos for his children's ministry.

Doris Holik Kelley

Doris Holik Kelly is an author and photographer who enjoys writing about historic places, persons, and legends. Doris has published five books. She and her husband hail from MI and . have two children, a granddaughter, and a grandson

Kathy L. Kuzas

Kathy L. Kuzas lives and works as her church's administrative secretary in northeastern Ohio. She is a mother and grandmother. Kathy has many hobbies and loves to read and travel.

Debbie Jordan

Debbie Jordan is a multifaceted chameleon who learned to adapt transition and adjust to life as a military wife of 22 years. Debbie and Dennis have been married for over 50 years. They enjoys traveling, hiking, and spending time with her adult children and seven grandchildren. Proving that age is not a limitation, Debbie and Dennis travel anywhere in the world the Lord sends them, and are marriage and grief coaches. She recently published "Grief Deception: 12 Lies Whispered to a Broken Heart"

Bette Lafferty

Bette is a widow of 14 years, she says writing has become her salvation, keeping her mind sharp while saving memories for her children, granddaughter,and friends. Bette is a punlished author of several bools. For over 16 years Bette has produced her *Monday Morning Offering* (poems and vignettes)for over 160 readers. It is her joy to share her work with others.

Dara Armstrong Lehner

Dara Armstrong Lehner is a writer, editor, publisher, and photographer. She lives in NC with her husband of 43 years. They are blessed with two children, six grandchildren, and three great-grandsons. Dara loves to write in both fiction and non-fiction genres. Her hobbies include flower and vegetable gardening, needlecraft, genealogy, and swimming.

Peter Lundell

Peter Lundell, D. Miss. is a professional editor, as well as pastor, college professor, and writer, who helps authors effectively write to publish their message. He writes and edits so that words are "smooth as silk, flow like water." Peter and his wife live on the West Coast.

Josephine "Jo" Massaro

Jo is a motivational speaker and author. She is the founder and CEO of In Their Hands, a nonprofit aimed to build community while increasing literacy. Jo worked as a paralegal and co-founded a non-profit with her husband to work with HIV/AIDS while living in New York. She lives in Northeast IN with her professional chef husband Dominic. They have five children and six incredible grandchildren.

C. Ben Mitchell

C. Ben Mitchell, PhD (University of Tennessee at Knoxville) is a semi-retired professor of bioethics and public policy and university administrator. Among other works, he is the author of *Ethics and Moral Reasoning: A Students Guide* (Crossway Publishers)

Crystal Murray

Crystal Murray is a Christian freelance writer. She is an active leader and volunteer at her church. She has been instrumental in encouraging and assisting other Christian writers through writing groups and conferences she is affiliated with. Crystal lives in SE Indiana with her husband, David.

Viloshinee Muragan

Viloshinee "Vee" Murugan grew up in South Africa during the Apartheid years. Vee comes from a family of educators. She has served 26 years in education in South Africa, London (UK), NC, and MI. Vee has a bachelor's in Pedagogic Education, and has post-graduate degrees in Environmental Education and Educational Leadership. Currently, Vee lives in MI with her daughter.

Tonie Neal

Tonie served as a middle school guidance counselor for 24 years in NC. She has been an active member of her church for almost 60 years, holding many leadership roles in church, civic, and charitable organizations. Tonie has three grown children. She currently lives in central NC with James, her husband of 48 years.

Charlotte Hunt Norris

Charlotte Hunt Norris is a retired elementary school music teacher. She recently retired as the director of the Music Ministry at her church, having served 65 years. Charlotte is a sought-after pianist and organist. Her daughter tragically died, but her two wonderful granddaughters survived. Charlotte and her husband, Rick, live in central Ohio.

Robert Ousnamer

Mr. Ousnamer studied technical theater, music education, and photography at Indiana University. He is the lead formatter and cover designer for a partnership publishing company with authors across the globe. Robert resides with his wife in Central Florida and enjoys their eight grandchildren, travel, camping, and model trains.

Dorothy Purge

Dorothy Purge writes children's literature, general interest articles, and edits. Her award-winning story " Wash Day" is a literary fiction. Dorothy was the recipient of a writing scholarship from Highlights Foundation for Children and the University of Glasgow MLit department. Dorothy uses photography as an essential tool in her writing. She is currently coordinating writing courses. Writers of importance to her include Alan Durant, Kwame Dawes, and her first writing tutor, Cecil 'Cec' Murphy. Dorothy also works in Human Resources.

Fran Caffey Sandin

Fran Caffey Sandin has published magazine articles in Decision, oody, Focus on the Family, and many others, contributed to twenty books, has ghost-written three books, and authored *See You Later, Jeffrey; Touching the Clouds: True Stories to Strengthen Your Faith;* and most recently, *HOPE on the Way: DEVOTIONS to Go.* She and her husband, Jim, are parents of two sons in Heaven, a beautiful daughter and son-in-law, and three fabulous grandchildren.

Ann Tantlinger

Ann is a retired teacher and writer. She was educated and taught in central Ohio. She and her husband, Ron, have retired to the beautiful Pennsylvania countryside and are building a new home. They have two adult sons, a daughter, and several grandchildren.

JoAnne Coble Woodard

JoAnne C. Woodard PhD is the proud Founder and Executive Director of the Sallie B. Howard School of Arts and Science and the YEP - Youth Enrichment Program (a summer program) in Wilson, NC. She has made it her life's work to cultivate the gifts, talents, and potential of children (and families) enabling them to become more than they thought they could.

Barbara Wright

Barbara Wright is currently a middle school Social Studies teacher for 25 years. Barbara is an honored three-time Teacher of the Year from her school.She is an only child and a great daughter to her mother who showed her the value of teaching by example. Barbara has a daughter and son and four grandchildren. She serves in her local church and loves God with all her heart.

www.ingramcontent.com/pod-product-compliance
Lightning Source LLC
Chambersburg PA
CBHW020456160726
47991CB00007B/2675